To: Julee
Thank you!
Michael Willis

The Gardener's Love

by Michael Wells
Illustrated by Karen Malzeke-McDonald

Thomas Nelson Publishers
Nashville • Atlanta • London • Vancouver

Published in Nashville, Tennessee, by Thomas Nelson, Inc., Publishers and distributed in Canada by Word Communications, Ltd., Richmond, British Columbia, and in the United Kingdom by Word (UK), Ltd., Milton Keynes, England.

Scripture quotations are from THE NEW KING JAMES VERSION of the Bible. Copyright © 1979, 1980, 1982, Thomas Nelson, Inc., Publishers.

Library of Congress Cataloging-in-Publication Data

Wells, Michael, 1952-
   The gardener's love / Michael Wells ; illustrated by Karen Malzeke-McDonald.
   p. cm.
ISBN 0-7852-7198-8 (hardcover)
   1. Christian life. I. Malzeke-McDonald, Karen. II. Title.
BV4501.2.W41815   1997
242--dc21   97-11217
                                                   CIP

Printed in the United States of America
1 2 3 4 5 6 7 — 03 02 01 00 99 98 97

The Gardener's Love

To the One apart from whom we can do nothing.
John 15:5

ALEX was a branch who lived in a vase. Alex had a problem. He had no life! Alex was cut off. Alex was dying, and he was very depressed.

Alex was surprised. The Gardener's touch was very gentle as he took Alex and began walking toward the Vine. It was the very Vine Alex had seen from the window.

The Gardener made a small cut in the Vine and placed Alex in it. Alex was very excited, but only for a moment.

He wanted genuine fruit. Fruit that comes from life. Life is QUIET, CALM, and very FRAGRANT. Not like a factory.

ALEX could see a living Vine with living branches and real fruit from the window's edge.

Alex was jealous.
He wanted to be like
living branches.
So he would never
give up!

He would strain and imitate. But he would die. Alex was depressed.

It was a sunny morning.

A stranger appeared, and

He was called the Gardener.

The Gardener approached Alex and took hold of him. Alex thought,

"I will now be thrown away."

ALEX could not help himself.

However, Alex would not give up trying!

Alex wanted life and he wanted fruit.

Not plastic fruit from a factory. Factories are LOUD, HOT, and they SMELL.

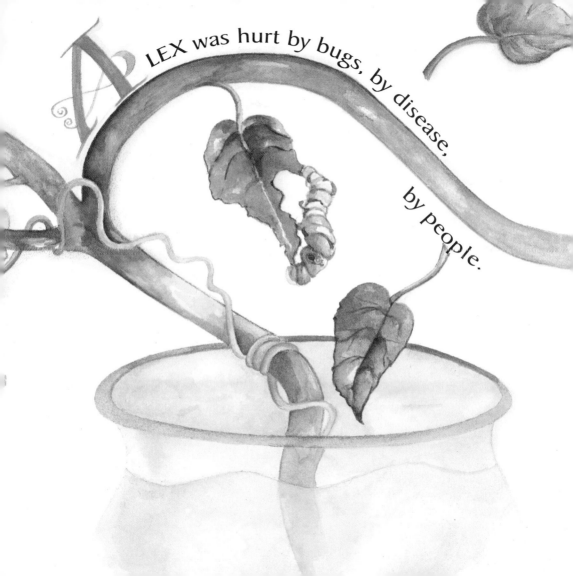

ALEX was hurt by bugs, by disease, by people.

ALEX wanted to be alive.

He worked, he strained,
he tried harder.
But Alex continued to die!

Alex tried to hold on to the Vine.
However, he could not.
By now Alex was very weak.
Alex was dying.

Alex had not expected what happened next. The Gardener held Alex in place while the living Vine took hold of him. At first, Alex was afraid that he would fall away from the Vine. However, once he felt the strength of the Vine…

Alex knew he had
nothing to fear.

New life began to flow into Alex.

He was no longer dying.

The Vine's life was CONFIDENT,

HEALING, and POWERFUL.

The Vine's life now belonged to Alex.

It was his life, too! Alex was very happy!

The Gardener loved the Vine and all that was attached to it. The Gardener loved Alex.

Alex was free from work, from strain, and from every care. The Gardener and the Vine took care of everything.

Early one morning Alex was awakened. Something was happening! A bud had formed on Alex...which became a flower...and finally turned to fruit!

Alex was bearing fruit!

NATURALLY!

Without effort! The life of the Vine had so filled Alex that the excess was flowing out.

Real fruit! Real fruit! Alex was really living. Fruit was everywhere and Alex was happy! Alex noticed how happy the fruit made the Gardener.

However, Alex was surprised to see that the Gardener did not want the fruit for Himself.

The Gardener gave the fruit to a very poor family.

The Gardener was happy.

The Vine was happy. This made Alex feel good, satisfied, and special. Alex continued to grow and become bigger and bigger.

ne day the Gardener approached the Vine with very sharp shears. Alex thought, "Many other branches will be trimmed today, but I shall not, for I have given the Gardener fruit."

But as the Gardener neared he turned toward Alex. The Gardener began cutting away all the shoots that bore the most fruit that year.

Alex protested, "Why cut away what is good? Why cut away the source of my gift to you?".

The Gardener spoke gently to Alex. "The source of your fruit was not your shoots but the Vine! You gave me nothing but what was given you. If the shoots are not cut away, the bigger they get, the more you will trust them and the less fruit they will give Me!"

The Gardener spoke again to Alex. "Today I will tell you a secret! A branch cannot hold on to the glory of the past season. You must allow Me to cut it away and make room for a new and greater glory to come."

Alex agreed. He was pruned. He grew stronger, and bore larger fruit.

Alex became a grand branch.

One day Alex saw something that disturbed him. In a distant window, a branch in a vase was dying.

Alex remembered the feeling of being cut off and dying. He was scared. He began to work once again to hold on to the Vine.

The Gardener noticed that Alex was no longer happy. He questioned him, "Alex, what has happened to all your joy?" Alex explained, "I never want to be cut off again, so I'm working harder and harder to hold on to the Vine."

The Gardener once again spoke softly. "Alex, were you firm in the branch because of your work?" Alex answered, "No." "Then now! I will keep you always! Without Me you can do nothing," said the Gardener.

Alex then decided to let the Gardener do his job of keeping, the Vine do his job of giving life, and he would be content to receive in order to give.

So Alex rested. He was happy.
And he bore more fruit.

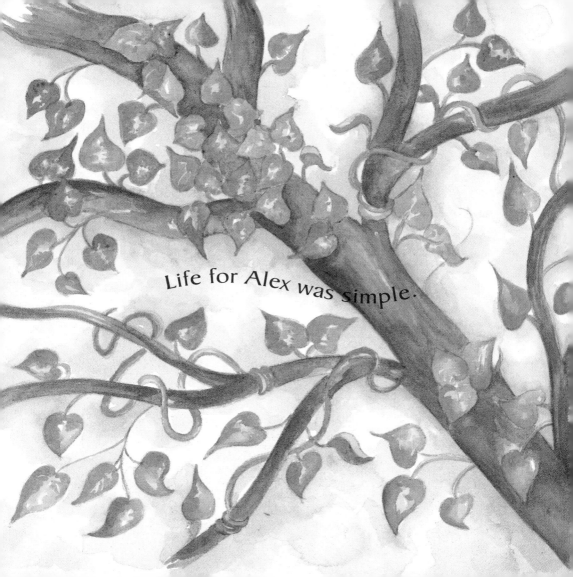

Life for Alex was simple.